Puffin Books

HOT DOG AND OTHER POEMS

Sometimes serious, sometimes silly, Kit Wright's long-awaited collection *Hot Dog* is one of the best new books of children's poetry to have appeared for many years. Completely modern in feeling and expression, and ranging over a wide variety of metre and form, the poems manage to transform even the most everyday experience into something note-worthy.

Kit Wright is particularly good on all the awful things that children have to endure: coping with stuck-up sisters and their boring boy-friends, being slobbered over by elderly relatives, or being made to tidy the bedroom. Even potentially sad situations are turned by his pen into joyful occasions: like the time when a disabled child comes into a crowded station waiting-room and suddenly makes all the disgruntled passengers cheerful.

And what a marvellous collection of characters run through the book! There's Dave Dirt and his dog, 'a horrible hound'; Walter Wall, the king of carpet salesmen; Uncle Laurie, who can't stop saying sorry; and the appalling Auntie Jean – all beautifully caught in Posy Simmonds's wickedly funny pictures.

Other books by Kit Wright

POEMS FOR 9-YEAR-OLDS AND UNDER
POEMS FOR OVER 10-YEAR-OLDS
CAT AMONG THE PIGEONS

Illustrated by Posy Simmonds

Kit Wright

HOT DOG

and Other Poems

Puffin Books

PUFFIN BOOKS

Published by the Penguin Group
Penguin Books Ltd, 27 Wrights Lane, London W8 5TZ, England
Penguin Books USA Inc., 375 Hudson Street, New York, New York 10014, USA
Penguin Books Australia Ltd, Ringwood, Victoria, Australia
Penguin Books Canada Ltd, 10 Alcorn Avenue, Toronto, Ontario, Canada M4V 3B2
Penguin Books (NZ) Ltd, 182–190 Wairau Road, Auckland 10, New Zealand

Penguin Books Ltd, Registered Offices: Harmondsworth, Middlesex, England

First published by Kestrel Books 1981
Published in Puffin Books 1982
10 9

Printed in England by Clays Ltd, St Ives plc
Set in Monotype Plantin

For B. P. Adams
and
Tom and Lizzie and Zoe

CONTENTS

7

HOT DOG

My Dad can't stand my sister's latest boyfriend.
Boring?

When he comes round, even the dog
Starts snoring.

Our hamster crawls back in beneath
His straw. *Dad grits his teeth*.

Our budgie

Folds his wings and shuts up shop.
Dad's eyelids drop.

Boring?

What he goes on about
Is Being A Vegetarian.
His line is 'Meat is Out'
And his line doesn't vary an
Inch. It goes like this:

GIVE HAMBURGERS A MISS!

EVERYONE IS MISTAKEN
WHO EVER EATS BACON!

THE ENTIRE WORLD SHOULD STOP
FANCYING A PORK CHOP!

He's utterly convinced
Of the evil of beef, minced.

If he were God, he'd damn
All lamb. And ham. And spam.

What's best, he says, for you
Is lentil-and-seaweed stew.

He feels all meals should be:

Lentil-and-seaweed
Stew for breakfast,
Seaweed-and-lentil
Stew for tea.

Oh, he's *sincere* all right:
You couldn't doubt it.

But why must he
Go on and on
And on and *on*
About it?

My Dad can't *stand* my sister's latest boyfriend.
Boring?

Last night I really thought
That Dad would hit him.
What happened was the dog
Woke up and bit him.

My sister was really mad.
They stormed out. Dad

Sat stroking the dog and murmuring
Over and over again,
'Who's a good boy, who's a good boy,

Who's a *good dog*, then?'

IT'S SPRING, IT'S SPRING

It's spring, it's spring –

when everyone sits round a roaring fire
telling ghost stories!

It's spring, it's spring –

when everyone sneaks into everyone else's yard
and bashes up their snowman!

It's spring, it's spring –

when the last dead leaves fall from the trees
and Granny falls off your toboggan!

It's spring, it's spring –

when you'd give your right arm
for a steaming hot bowl of soup!

It's spring, it's spring –

when you'd give your right leg
not to be made to wash up after Christmas dinner!

It's spring, it's spring –

isn't it?

HEADS OR TAILS?

Dave Dirt's dog is a horrible hound,
    A hideous sight to see.
When Dave first brought it home from the pound,
We couldn't be certain which way round
    The thing was supposed to be!

Somebody said, 'If that's its *head*,
    It's *far* the ugliest dog in town.'
Somebody said, 'The darned thing's *dead*!'
    'Don't be silly, it's *upside-down*!'
'It's *inside-out*!' 'It's a sort of *plant*!'
'It's wearing *clothes*!' 'It's Dave Dirt's *aunt*!'
    'It's a sort of *dressing-gown*!'

Each expert had his own idea
    Of what it was meant to be
But everybody was far from clear –
    And yet. . .we *did* agree
That Dave Dirt's dog was a horrible hound
    And a hideous sight to see!

It *loves Dave Dirt*. It follows him round
    Through rain and sun and snow.
When set in motion, it looks far *worse*,
And nobody knows if it's in reverse
    Or the way it's supposed to go!

THE SONG OF THE WHALE

Heaving mountain in the sea,
Whale, I heard you
Grieving.

Great whale, crying for your life,
Crying for your kind, I knew
How we would use
Your dying:

Lipstick for our painted faces,
Polish for our shoes.

Tumbling mountain in the sea,
Whale, I heard you
Calling.

Bird-high notes, keening, soaring:
At their edge a tiny drum
Like a heartbeat.

We would make you
Dumb.

In the forest of the sea,
Whale, I heard you
Singing,

Singing to your kind.
We'll never let you be.
Instead of life we choose

Lipstick for our painted faces,
Polish for our shoes.

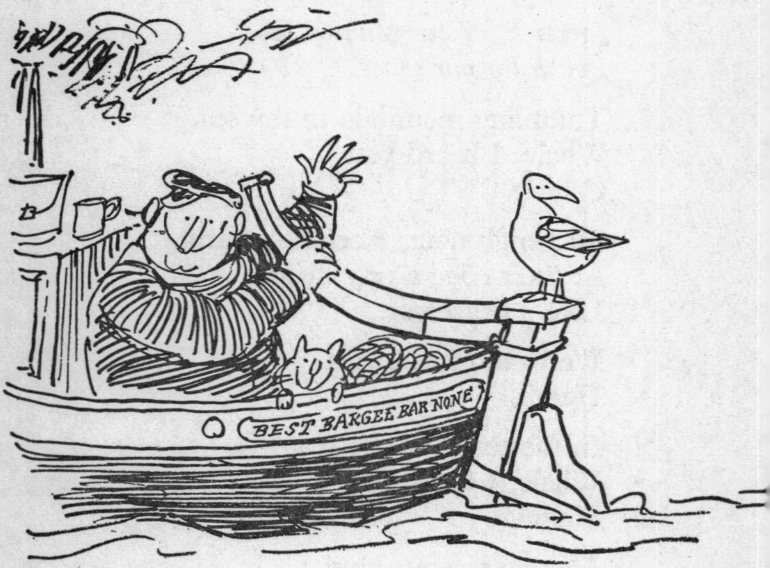
BEST BARGEE BAR NONE

SONG SUNG BY A MAN ON A BARGE TO ANOTHER MAN ON A DIFFERENT BARGE IN ORDER TO DRIVE HIM MAD

Oh,

I am the best bargee bar none,
You are the best bargee bar one!
You are the second-best bargee,
You are the best bargee bar me!

Oh,

I am the best . . .

(and so on, until he is
hurled into the canal)

USEFUL PERSON

We'd missed the train. Two hours to wait
On Lime Street Station, Liverpool,
With *not a single thing to do*.
The bar was shut and Dad was blue
And Mum was getting in a state
And everybody felt a fool.

Yes, we were very glum indeed.
Myself, I'd nothing new to read,
No sweets to eat, no game to play.
'I'm bored,' I said, and straight away,
Mum said what I knew she'd say:
'Go on, then, read a book, O.K.?'
'I've *read* them *both*!' 'That's no excuse.'

Dad sat sighing, '*What* a day . . .
This is precious little use.
I wish they'd open up that bar.'
They didn't, though. No way.

And everybody else was sitting
In that waiting-room and knitting,
Staring, scratching, yawning, smoking.
'All right, Dad?' 'You must be joking!
This is precious little use.
It's like a prison. Turn me loose!'

('Big fool, act your age!' Mum hisses.
'Sorry, missus.'
'Worse than him, you are,' said Mum.)

It was grim. It was glum.

And then the Down's syndrome child came up,
Funny-faced:
Something in her body wrong,
Something in her mind
Misplaced:
Something in her eyes was strange:
What, or why, I couldn't tell:
But somehow she was beautiful
As well.

Anyway, she took us over!
'Hello, love,' said Dad. She said,
'*There*, sit *there*!' and punched a spot
On the seat. The spot was what,
Almost, Mum was sitting on,
So Dad squeezed up, and head-to-head,
And crushed-up, hip-to-hip, they sat.
'What next, then?' 'Kiss!' 'Oh no, not that!'
Dad said, chuckling. '*Kiss!*'

                      They did!

I thought my Mum would flip her lid
With laughing. Then the Down's syndrome child
Was filled with pleasure – she went wild,
Running round the tables, telling
Everyone to *kiss* and yelling
Out to everyone to sit
Where she said. They did, too. It

Was sudden happiness because
The Down's syndrome child
Was what she was:
Bossy, happy, full of fun,
And just *determined* everyone
Should have a good time too! We knew
That's what we'd got to do.

Goodness me, she took us over!
All the passengers for Dover,
Wolverhampton, London, Crewe –
Everyone from everywhere
Began to share
Her point of view! The more they squeezed,
And laughed, and fooled about, the more
The Down's syndrome child
Was pleased!

Dad had to kiss another Dad
('Watch it, lad!' '*You* watch it, lad!'
'Stop: you're not my kind of bloke!')
Laugh? I thought that Mum would choke!

And so the time whirled by. The train
Whizzed us home again
And on the way I thought of her:

Precious little use is what
Things had been. Then she came
And things were not
The same!

She was precious, she was little,
She was useful too:
Made us speak when we were dumb,
Made us smile when we were blue,
Cheered us up when we were glum,
Lifted us when we were flat:
Who could be
More use than that?

Down's syndrome child,
Funny-faced,
Something in your body wrong,
Something in your mind
Misplaced,
Something in your eyes, strange:
What, or why, I cannot tell:
I thought you were beautiful:

Useful, as well.

THE RABBIT'S CHRISTMAS CAROL

I'm sick as a parrot,
I've lost me carrot,
I couldn't care less if it's
Christmas Day.

I'm sick as a parrot,
I've lost me carrot,
So get us a lettuce
Or . . . go away!

DREADFUL DREAM

I'm glad to say
I've never met
A cannibal
And yet

In this dream
I had last night
I almost took
A bite

Of somebody
Or other who
Was standing in
A stew-

Pot full of water
On a batch
Of firewood. Just
One match

Would do to start
It off. Whereat
I hollered, 'Just
Stop that!'

But cannibals
Began to shout:
'You've got to try
Him out!'

'Who? Me?' 'That's right.'
'I'd rather not,'
I said. They yelled,
'You've *got*

To have a taste!
Don't *want* to?' 'Not,'
I answered them,
'A lot,

Since, now you put
Me on the spot,
*He wouldn't taste
So hot.*'

At this the chap
Who'd soon be stewed
Remarked, 'I call
That *rude*!

Most ungrateful!
Here I am –
About to be
A ham –

Just to *please* you!
"WHAT A TREAT",
Not "HE'S UNFIT
TO EAT",

Is what I'd hoped
To hear. Well, stuff
It then, I've had
Enough.'

And out he stepped
As bold as day,
Shook-dried and stalked
Away.

The cannibals got
Quite excited:
'Last time *you're*
Invited!

Could have had him
On a bun:
Now look what
You've done!

Hurt his feelings,
BUNGLEHEAD!
We'll eat *you*
Instead.'

Things had got
Beyond a joke.
Thank goodness I
Awoke.

Dreadful dream!
Next time I sleep
I plan to do
It deep.

GREEDYGUTS

I sat in the café and sipped at a Coke.
There sat down beside me a WHOPPING great bloke
Who sighed as he elbowed me into the wall:
'Your trouble, my boy, is your belly's too small!
Your bottom's too thin! Take a lesson from me:
I may not be nice, but I'm GREAT, you'll agree,
And I've lasted a lifetime by playing this hunch:
The bigger the breakfast, the larger the lunch!

The larger the lunch, then the huger the supper.
The deeper the teapot, the vaster the cupper.
The fatter the sausage, the fuller the tea.
The MORE on the table, the BETTER for ME!'

His elbows moved in and his elbows moved out,
His belly grew bigger, chins wobbled about,
As forkful by forkful and plate after plate,
He ate and he ate and he ate and he ATE!

I hardly could breathe, I was squashed out of shape,
So under the table I made my escape.

'Aha!' he rejoiced, 'when it's put to the test,
The fellow who's fattest will come off the best!
Remember, my boy, when it comes to the crunch:
The bigger the breakfast, the larger the lunch!

The larger the lunch, then the huger the supper.
The deeper the teapot, the vaster the cupper.
The fatter the sausage, the fuller the tea.
The MORE on the table, the BETTER for ME!'

A lady came by who was scrubbing the floor
With a mop and a bucket. To even the score,
I lifted that bucket of water and said,
As I poured the whole lot of it over his head:

'*I've* found all my life, it's a pretty sure bet:
The FULLER the bucket, the WETTER you GET!'

GOBBLING AND SQUABBLING

In a very old house
On a street full of cobbles,
Two very old ladies
Have got colly-wobbles,

And out on the pavement
The neighbours are grumbling,
And sighing, 'Oh *when* will
Their stomachs stop rumbling?'

THE BUDGIE'S NEW YEAR MESSAGE

Get a little tin of bird-seed,
Pour it in my little trough.
If you don't, you little twit, I'll
Bite your little finger off!

HUGGER MUGGER

I'd sooner be
Jumped and thumped and dumped,

I'd sooner be
Slugged and mugged . . . than *hugged* . . .

And clobbered with a slobbering
Kiss by my Auntie Jean:

You know what I mean:

Whenever she comes to stay,
You know you're bound

To get one.
A quick
  short
  peck
  would
  be
  O.K.
But this is a
Whacking great
Smacking great
Wet one!

All whoosh and spit
And crunch and squeeze
And 'Dear little boy!'
And 'Auntie's missed you!'
And 'Come to Auntie, she
Hasn't kissed you!'
Please don't do it, Auntie,
PLEASE!

Or if you've absolutely
Got to,

And nothing on earth can persuade you
Not to,

The trick
Is to make it
Quick,

You know what I mean?

For as things are,
I really would far,

Far sooner be
Jumped and thumped and dumped,

I'd sooner be
Slugged and mugged . . . than hugged . . .

And clobbered with a slobbering
Kiss by my Auntie

Jean!

38

WHERE THE FLOWERS WENT

Where have all the flowers gone,
The flowers that were standing on
The grave beside the churchyard wall?
  My little brother grabbed them

And stuffed them in an old tin can
And took them home to give my Gran,
Who wasn't very pleased at all –
  'Tell me where you nabbed them!'

Then out they crept
As quiet as mice

To put them back
Without being caught:

'It's *wrong*,' said Gran,
'But still the thought

Was

Nice!'

WATCH OUT, WALTER WALL!

The king of carpet salesmen
  Is a man called Walter Wall.
He's got a shop next door to us
  He used to think too small.
And so he asked permission, please,
  To *alter* WALTER WALL.

'What? Alter WALTER WALL?' the Council
  Cried. 'Why? What's the call?'
'My rugs are filling up with bugs
  From standing in the hall.
My place has got no stacking-space –
  No space,' said Walt, 'at all!'

The Council said, 'Go right ahead.
  Don't falter, Walter Wall!
It's alteration stations, Walter.
  Sideways, build a tall
Extension, that will form an extra
  Wall to WALTER WALL!'

And so across the taller wall
  I call to Walter Wall
And over it I often boot
  A ball to Walter Wall.
Likewise the cat can crawl the wall
  And *fall* to Walter Wall!

So everything has worked out well:
  More space for Walter Wall.
The cat and I have got a place
  To crawl, fall, boot a ball:

And often, I am proud to say,
  The cat and ball, instead
Of landing on the carpets, clout
  Old Walt *hard* on the head!

HOW TO TREAT THE HOUSE-PLANTS

All she ever thinks about are house-plants.
She talks to them and tends them every day.
And she says, 'Don't hurt their feelings. Give them
Love. In all your dealings with them,
Treat them in a tender, *human* way.'

'Certainly, my dear,' he says. 'O.K.
Human, eh?'

But the house-plants do not seem to want to play.

They are stooping, they are drooping,
They are kneeling in their clay:
They are flaking, they are moulting,
Turning yellow, turning grey,
And they look . . . well, quite revolting
As they sigh, and fade away.

So after she has left the house he gets them
And he sets them in a line against the wall,
And I cannot say he cossets them or pets them –
No, he doesn't sympathize with them at all.
Is he tender? Is he human? Not a bit.
No, to each of them in turn he says: 'You *twit*!

You're a
    Rotten little skiver,
    Cost a fiver,
    Earn your keep!

You're a
    Dirty little drop-out!
    You're a cop-out!
    You're a creep!

You're a
    Mangy little whinger!
    You're a cringer!
    Son, it's true –

    I have justbin
    To the dustbin
    Where there's *better men than you*!

    Get that stem back!

    Pull your weight!

    Stick your leaves out!

    STAND UP STRAIGHT!'

And, strange to say, the plants co-operate.
So when she comes back home and finds them glowing,
Green and healthy, every one a king,
She says, 'It's *tenderness* that gets them growing!
How strange, the change a little *love* can bring!'

'Oh yes,' he says. 'Not half. Right. Love's the thing.'

THE CATCH

You'll receive a
Vauxhall Viva
if you win our
competition:

oh, well done, sir,
you have won, sir,
here's the keys to
the ignition:

off you go now,
take it slow, now,
MIND OUR WALL –
oh dear, a skid, sir:

what a spill, sir,
here's our bill, sir:
you owe *us*
a thousand quid, sir!

BABBLING AND GABBLING

My Granny's an absolute corker,
My Granny's an absolute cracker,
But she's Britain's speediest talker
And champion yackety-yacker!

Everyone's fond of my Granny,
Everyone thinks she's nice,
But before you can say Jack Robinson,
My Granny's said it twice!

THE ROVERS

My Dad, he wears a Rovers' scarf,
He wears a Rovers' cap,
And every Saturday before
He goes to see them fail to score,
    He sighs, 'Oh no!
    Why *do* I go?
    They haven't got –
    They've really not –
A rat's chance in a trap!'

And sure enough
They always stuff
    The Rovers.

My Dad, he wears a Rovers' tie,
    Two huge rosettes as well,
And every time before he leaves
He sits and hangs his head and grieves:

'I must be mad –
    They're just so BAD!
    They haven't got –
    They've really not –
A snowball's hope in hell!'

And sure enough
They always stuff
  The Rovers.

Rovers' ribbon, Rovers' rattle,
Dad takes when he's off to battle:
Shouts and stamps and stomps and rants.
DAD'S GOT ROVERS' UNDERPANTS!

Rovers' eyes!
Rovers' nose!
Rovers' elbows!
Off he goes

  And sure enough
  They always stuff
    The Rovers.

EXCEPT
One glorious day,
It didn't work that way . . .
This was the state of play . . .

  A goal-less draw,
  But just before
  The final whistle went,
  Rovers stole
  The only goal:
  I can't say it was *meant*:

What happened was
A wobbling cross
Back-bounced off someone's bum –
And Praise the Lord!
Rovers scored!
They'd won! Their hour had come!

So Dad, he whirled his Rovers' scarf,
    He hurled his cap up high.
'Oh, we're the best there's ever been!
We're magic!' he yelled out. 'You've seen
        Nothing yet.
        Just wait. We're set!
        Yes, you can bet
        The lads will get
    Promotion by and by!

Our luck is in –
We're *bound* to win –
        Us Rovers!'

It didn't work that way,
Alas for Dad.
That goal's the only goal
They've ever had.

Now every Saturday before
He goes to see them lose once more,
He sighs, 'Oh no!
Why *do* I go?
They've got a curse –
They're getting *worse* –
How *can* they be so bad?'

And sure enough
They always
STUFF THE ROVERS!

PRIDE

Two birds sat in a Big White Bra
   That swung as it hung
   On the washing-line.

They sang: 'Hurray!' and they sang: 'Hurrah!
Of all the birds we're the best by far!
Our hammock swings to the highest star!
   No life like yours and mine!'

They were overheard
   By a third
   Bird

That swooped down on to a nearby tree
And sneered: 'Knickers! It's plain to see
A bird in a tree is worth two in a bra.
   There's no bird *half* so fine!'

And it seemed indeed that he was right
For the washing-line was *far* too tight
And old and frayed. As the laundry flapped,
The big wind heaved and the rope . . . *snapped*!

You should have heard
  The third
  Bird.

He cried: 'Aha!
For all their chatter and la-de-dah,
They didn't get far in their Big White Bra!
If there *is* a bird who's a Superstar,
It's me, it's me, it's me!'

Down to the ground
He dived in his glee

And the Big Black Cat
Enjoyed his tea.

IN THE CATHEDRAL GARDENS

In the Cathedral Gardens
Underneath the trees

In the chilly evening
The sun is on its knees,

Dying by the gravestones
While their shadows freeze

And the dead are walking
Underneath the trees.

THE GREAT DETECTIVE

Oh, I am the greatest detective
  The criminal world's ever known,
For my eyesight is never defective
  And my ears are entirely my own.

I've never been stuck for an answer,
  I've never been troubled by doubt,
Dismay or confusion: I form my conclusion
  By sorting the evidence out.

Last night I came home. As I entered,
  I straight away lighted upon
The fact that the telly was off from the way
  I could see that the thing wasn't on!

I noticed a man in there, *sitting* . . .
  A man that, I know, sometimes stands.
I could tell by one look he was reading a book
  From the book that he held in his hands!

I heard a voice call from the landing.
  It wasn't my sister or brother.
I could tell that the voice was my own mother's voice
  Since the voice was the voice of my mother!

It shouted, 'Get up here and tidy
  Your bedroom!' The man who sat reading
Made no move at all in response to the call,
  Neither left foot nor right foot proceeding.

A curious case. I imagined
  Some sort of a misunderstanding.
That the yell came again I knew instantly when
  The yell came again from the landing

Highly suspicious. The evidence
  Seemed to me, nonetheless, thin.
Tiptoeing the floor, I departed once more
  By the very same door I'd come in.

Yes, I am the greatest detective
  The criminal world's ever known,
For my eyesight is never defective
  And my ears are entirely my own.

SAY 'AAGH!'

No fun being the dentist.
  Not much fun as a job:
Spending all of your days in gazing
  Right into everyone's gob.

No fun *seeing* the dentist.
  Not much fun at all:
Staring straight up his hairy nostrils –
  Drives you up the wall!

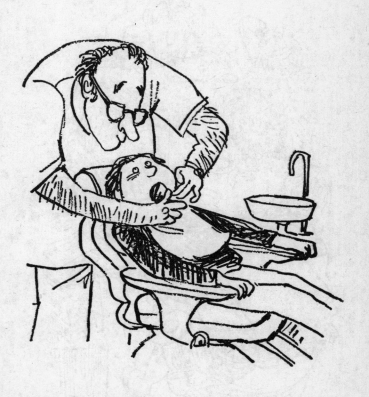

DAVE DIRT CAME TO DINNER

Dave Dirt came to dinner
    And he stuck his chewing gum
Underneath the table
    And it didn't please my Mum

And it didn't please my Granny
    Who was quite a sight to see
When she got up from the table
    With the gum stuck to her knee

Where she put her cup and saucer
    When she sat and drank her tea
And the saucer and the chewing gum
    Got stuck as stuck can be

And she staggered round the kitchen
    With a saucer on her skirt –
No, it didn't please my Granny
    But it
            PLEASED
                DAVE
                DIRT

HUNDREDS AND THOUSANDS

Under the hair-drier,
Under the hair,

The head of my sister
Is dreaming of where

She sits by the sea-shore
On somebody's yacht,

Drinking and thinking
And dreaming of what

She'll buy with her hundreds
And thousands of dollars,

Like ten silver tom-cats
With golden flea-collars

To yawn round the lawn
Of her garden in France

Where she lies by the pool
As the blue ripples dance,

And millions of brilliant
People dive in,

All loaded with money
And honey and gin,

All wonderfully funny
With witty remarks

As the sun in the water
Makes shivering sparks

And there by the pool
She lies browning and basking as

All of the people cry,
'Thank you for asking us!'

That's what I read
In her dopy sea-stare

Under the hair-drier,
Under the hair.

She wakes from her dreaming
Of making a mint

And – *would you believe it?* –
She's UTTERLY SKINT!

She's stealing all *my*
Pocket money from *me*!

'I'm off to the Disco –
Need 20 more p!'

CLEANING LADIES

Belly stuffed with dust and fluff,
    The Hoover moos and drones,
Grazing down on the carpet pasture:
    Cow with electric bones.

Up in the tree of a chair the cat
    Switches off its purr,
Stretches, blinks: a neat pink tongue
    Vacuum-cleans its fur.

LAURIE AND DORRIE

The first thing that you'll notice if
  You meet my Uncle Laurie
Is how, whatever else he does,
  He can't stop saying sorry.

He springs from bed at 5 a.m.
  As birds begin to waken,
Cries, 'No offence intended, lads –
  Likewise, I hope, none taken!'

This drives his wife, my Auntie Dorrie,
  Mad. It's not surprising
She grabs him by the throat and screeches,
  'Stop apologizing!'

My Uncle, who's a little deaf,
　　Says, 'Sorry? Sorry, Dorrie?'
'For goodness' sake,' Aunt Dorrie screams,
　　'Stop saying sorry, Laurie!'

'Sorry, dear? Stop saying what?'
　　'SORRY!' Laurie's shaken.
'No need to be, my dear,' he says,
　　'For *no offence is taken*.

Likewise I'm sure that there was none
　　Intended on your part.'
'Dear Lord,' Aunt Dorrie breathes, 'what can
　　I do, where do I start?'

Then, 'Oh, I *see*,' says Uncle L.,
　　'You mean "stop saying sorry"!
I'm sorry to have caused offence –
　　Oops! Er . . . *sorry*, Dorrie!'

EATING CHEAPLY

You can eat, if you are plucky,
Though you've not 1 p to spend.

Simply order hot fried chucky
For yourself and for your friend,

And complain: 'THIS CHICKEN'S MUCKY!
It's disgusting! It's the end!

It's uneatable! It's yucky!
You can't *seriously* pretend

This is *food*? Why, you'd be lucky
If a *rat* would eat it! Send

The lot back to the chuckery
Where it came from! I intend

To report this matter, ducky:
That means CURTAINS, FINISH, END!'

But

All the time you're knocking it,
Keep wolfing it. Make sure
You've bolted all the chicken down –

THEN

Bolt out through the door!

IT'S WINTER, IT'S WINTER

It's winter, it's winter, it's wonderful winter,
When everyone lounges around in the sun!

It's winter, it's winter, it's wonderful winter,
When everyone's brown like a steak overdone!

It's winter, it's winter, it's wonderful winter,
It's swimming and surfing and hunting for conkers!

It's winter, it's winter, it's wonderful winter,
And I am completely and utterly bonkers!

HOW I SEE IT

Some say the world's
A hopeless case:
A speck of dust
In all that space.
It's certainly
A scruffy place.
Just one hope
For the human race
That I can see:
Me. I'm
ACE!

WOULDN'T YOU LIKE TO KNOW

Michael Rosen

A collection of over 40 poems, including several specially written for this Puffin edition. Michael Rosen has a regular children's poetry column in the *Sunday Times* colour magazine.

I LIKE THIS POEM

edited by Kaye Webb

A unique collection of poems chosen by children for children, published in aid of the International Year of the Child.

YOU TELL ME

Roger McGough and Michael Rosen

A collection of largely humorous poems by two well-known poets – it's one of the funniest, most exciting books of poetry you're ever likely to read.

THE PUFFIN BOOK OF MAGIC VERSE

edited by Charles Causley

All poetry is magic. This far-ranging anthology includes incantations and curses, poems about elves, changelings, wizards, ghosts and mermaids, but also on the mystery and magic of the natural world and everyday life.

THE PUFFIN BOOK OF SALT-SEA VERSE

edited by Charles Causley

Here are poems about sailors, fish and fisherfolk, ships, storms, dreams and treasures, and above all about the wild and masterful ocean itself.

FIGGIE HOBBIN

Charles Causley

One of the most popular books of poems for children to have been produced in the last decade, the wide-ranging contents have a strong Cornish flavour.

POEMS FOR 7-YEAR-OLDS AND UNDER

chosen by Helen Nicoll

An inviting collection of poems, both old and modern, which makes a perfect introduction to the fun of poetry. Among sing-song limericks and boisterous verses from such favourites as Spike Milligan, Lewis Carroll and Roald Dahl, are poignant and magical poems from Robert Frost, Walter de la Mare and John Clare. A classic anthology that will surprise, delight and stimulate young readers.

SEA IN MY MIND

Selected poems from the *Observer* National Children's Poetry Competition

This collection of remarkable poetry by children covers a wide range of subjects from love and loss, to people and places, from birds and beasts, to wind and water. Chosen from top entries and award winners in the *Observer* National Children's Poetry Competition, this selection is an enlightening and enjoyable look at the world by young people today.

THE SUN, DANCING

edited by Charles Causley

A collection of light and imaginative Christian verse, produced from over a thousand years. This book is particularly useful as a reference book for either the home or the school library.

PLEASE MRS BUTLER
Janet and Allan Ahlberg

A funny collection of poems all about one school. The verses cover such things as playtime, the school outing, French lessons, best friends and a host of other topics within the school context.

DUCKS AND DRAGONS
edited by Gene Kemp

Children take to poetry like ducks to water, says Gene Kemp in the introduction to her anthology. A wide variety of poems, all tried and tested in the classroom.

ONCE UPON A RHYME
edited by Sara and Stephen Corrin

Well-known for their popular anthologies, the Corrins have now made their first collection of lighthearted verse for children who have progressed beyond nursery rhymes.

POETS IN HAND: A Puffin Quintet

edited by Anne Harvey

This book comprises the work for children of five highly respected British poets: Vernon Scannell, John Walsh, John Fuller, Elizabeth Jennings and Charles Causley.

A SINGLE STAR

edited by David Davis

A treasure-house of poems, songs and carols that contain between them all the joy and excitement of a real Christmas.

UNSPUN SOCKS FROM A CHICKEN'S LAUNDRY

Spike Milligan

A collection of new poems by the master of zany lyric. Illustrated throughout with drawings by Spike and his daughter.

GARGLING WITH JELLY

Brian Patten

A wonderful collection of poems, mostly funny, one or two serious, but all with something to make readers think twice, and perhaps change their views of life as a result.

NINE O'CLOCK BELL

edited by Raymond Wilson

A collection of poems about school for children of eight to twelve.

QUICK, LET'S GET OUT OF HERE!

Michael Rosen

A collection of poems about humorous, odd and real situations.